Studio 1:1

Architecture Under the Radar — Three Projects in Asia

Studio 1:1

Architecture Under the Radar
Three Projects in Asia

Foreword by **Nader Tehrani**
Afterword by **Gene Miao**

OSCAR RIERA OJEDA
PUBLISHERS

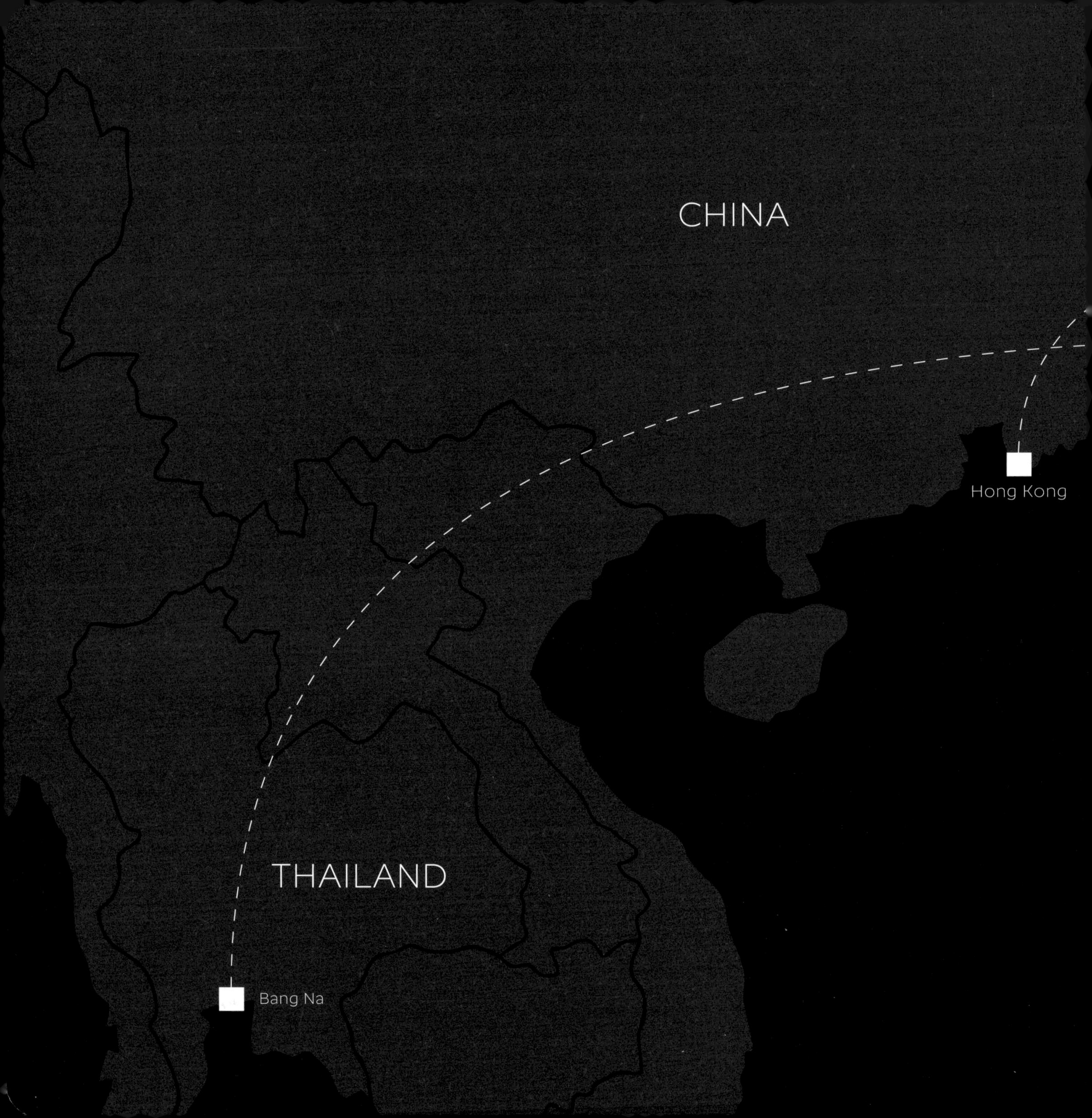
CHINA
Hong Kong
THAILAND
Bang Na

Mariveles
PHILIPPINES

Studio 1:1 of Refined Infrastructures

Nader Tehrani, 2024

Establishing an architectural voice is a daunting process, fraught with the imperative of creating a body of work as evidence, the consistency of voice it requires, a position that emerges out of it, and a relevance that situates it within a particular history. With a limited oeuvre, the weight of this task may seem even more daunting, and yet the work of Studio 1:1 gives this writer all the necessary clues to allow that voice to emerge.

The prospect of grouping disparate programs will not do that; a retail project, an entrance pavilion, and a manufacturing facility do not affiliate through common functions. Yet, in a poignant way, Gene Miao of Studio 1:1 brings them into conversation through the identification of infrastructures at different scales, occasions, and price-points. Behind the theme of infrastructure is the question of irreducibility, the ability to identify what might be the irrefutable and salient aspects of a given project—in effect, editing out all else. The infrastructure might be an engine without the shell of the car or the sail and rudder with no hull, but it makes sure to establish the key elements that allow an idea to thrive. If this were not a financial imperative for any given commission, I think it is even more vital as a disciplinary question. At a cultural moment when so many extraordinary architectural feats can be accomplished, it offers self-induced constraints as a gauge for critical thinking.

To be clear, there is no lack of exuberance in the work of Studio 1:1, quite the opposite. At first glance, the concomitant presence of craft and figuration points to a visual opulence that can even be misinterpreted as excess. However, upon closer inspection, the eye picks up on not the added layers of architecture, but rather the denuding of it: the careful elimination of surfaces that reveal layers of raw facts underneath.

Within the context of retail, where the quest for branding commonly results in boundless layers of added finishes, the dominant trope of **Muse Edition** (Page 30) is the celebration of the building's existing infrastructure, its coffered ceiling, steel columns, and with that the exposure of copper conduits delicately composed to transcend the terms of their functions. The structural coffering above maintains a vital function, as it supports a ballroom and swimming pool with considerable live loads, but the glass framing of the steel columns produces the ghost of figural "pilotis" that, at once, recall the monumentality of the structural effort in dialogue with the delicacy of casework, as if these steel members were jewels in need of curatorial identification. The exposure of these elements is further enhanced by the composition of infrastructure overhead; no longer merely at the service of electricity, these conduits conspire with mechanical diffusers to become figurative protagonists when they would otherwise be relegated to a reflective ceiling plan of suspended panels.

The **Entrance Pavilion** (Page 58) requires no accommodation for existing conditions as such, except for the road and vehicular infrastructure that is its host. In effect, the pavilion serves as a threshold between the larger metropolitan areas and the immediate community it supports, a virtual archway spanning the entry. Its conceit is not so much in its structure, but in how the form of its structure is evacuated of mass to serve as a liner for the programs it houses: lanterns over the roadway, as well as services and a security booth at its base. The thinness of its concrete structure belies the expectations of the normative girth required of spanning elements, and in turn, the sleight of hand is situated in how infrastructure and structure communicate with each other through the delicacy of a refined single line: a concrete shell that serves as an illuminated substrate for the very programs it houses. Critically, the lanterns are not so much suspended fixtures as extensions of the arches themselves: they allow the arches to frame the void whose space allows for the light to emanate on either side of the gate.

Of the triad, the **Light & Span** (Page 8) is possibly the most rough and tumble, a true factory. Composed of a column grid with long-span trusses held aloft, the idea of the building --in service of the workers it houses, is to bring the prospect of structure, daylighting, and hydrology into confluence. Of the three projects, it appears to be the most direct, and yet the landscape of the roof, composed of a field of scissor-trusses, produces a rhetoric so persuasive that it appears to float. Spanning some 36 meters each, the slippages between each bay allow for the scissors to lock, engaging the skylights, while allowing the water to drain against the column bays. Viewed as a whole, the roof appears as a winged flock, flying in unison floating above the workspace. Actual structure, delicately threaded into each other, it is ultimately the image of levity that renders it so seductive. Rough as a specification, the project retains a refinement both conceptual and visual: delicate in both language and proportions, it manifests as the definition of infrastructure itself.

With these works, Studio 1:1 displays not only protean latitude, but conceptual agility. Youthful in their linguistic play yet mature in how confidently they engage complex spatial, technological, and material assemblies, the continuity of an intellectual project seeps through. For me, it is not only a pleasure to prepare this introduction but also an acknowledgment of the necessary longevity of a pedagogical dialogue, a conversation launched in Providence decades ago, with hopefully many more to come around the world.

Light & Span

We worked closely with the engineer and contractor to develop a complex truss system for the roof design, resulting in a system of diamond-shaped skylights with a span of 36 meters. To simultaneously increase safety for the workers, reduce the weight of the roof, and control the budget, we specified polycarbonate panels (instead of glass) for the skylights on the roof. For the roof construction, off-the-shelf steel angles are welded to create steel frames, which are then welded together to form trusses. The construction method and technique for the roof is simple to the point of being primitive. Still, the result is a rather delicate and intricate framework that spans a vast interior space, allowing sufficient ambient daylight to filter in. The roof seems to be floating weightlessly and effortlessly above the workers. To combat heat gain through the skylights, we provided a series of large industrial fans to cool the interior space.

Type
Manufacturing Facility

Year
2016 - 2017

Area
6,750 sq.m

Material
Steel (Primary Building Material)

Address
Mariveles, Bataan, The Philippines

Objective
To create an improved working environment for the workers, and to create the longest span possible so that the client can attain greater flexibility in planning and setting up their production line within the facility.

Interior view of one of the pre-existing facilities on the premises. As you can see there is very little natural light entering the vast interior space.

Project Location

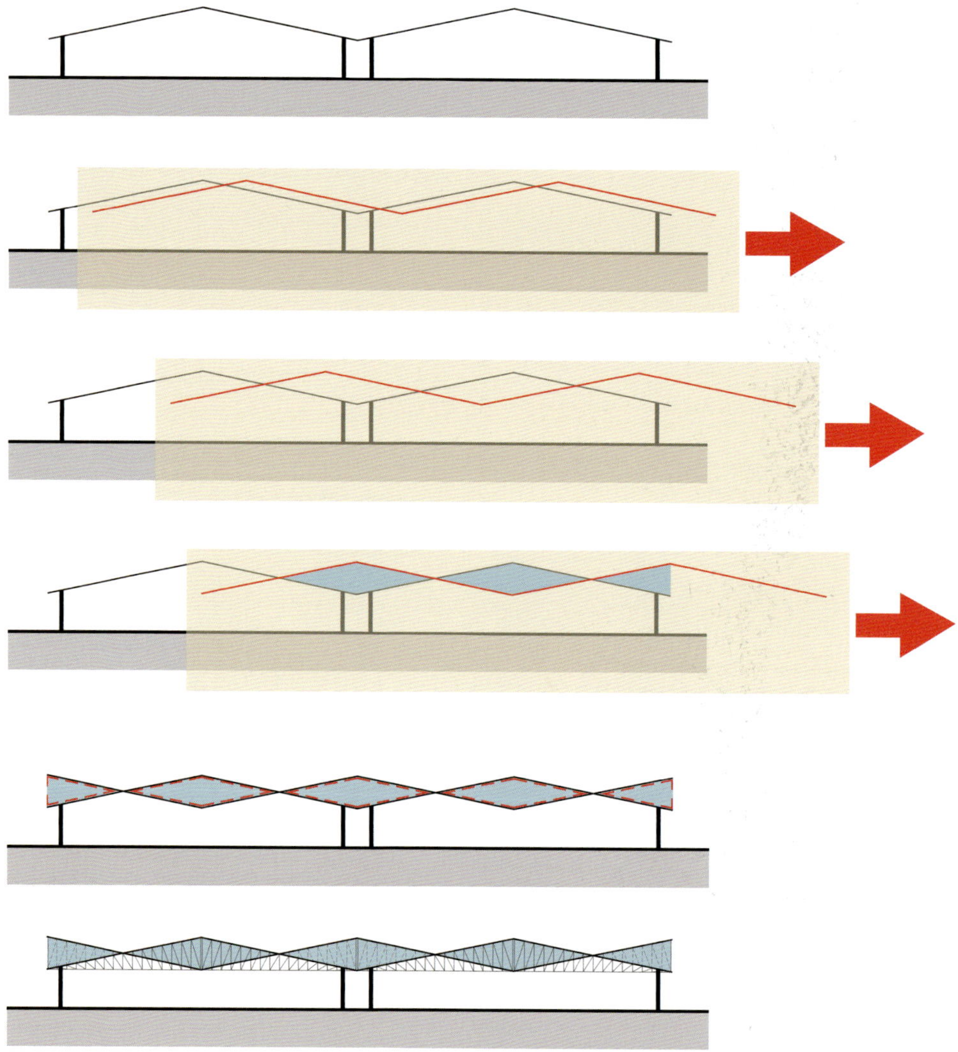

Sectional diagrams showing the development of the roof line and the diamond-shaped skylights.

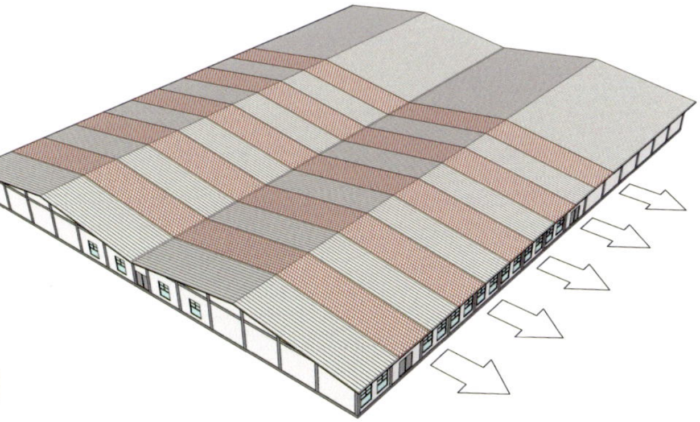

1

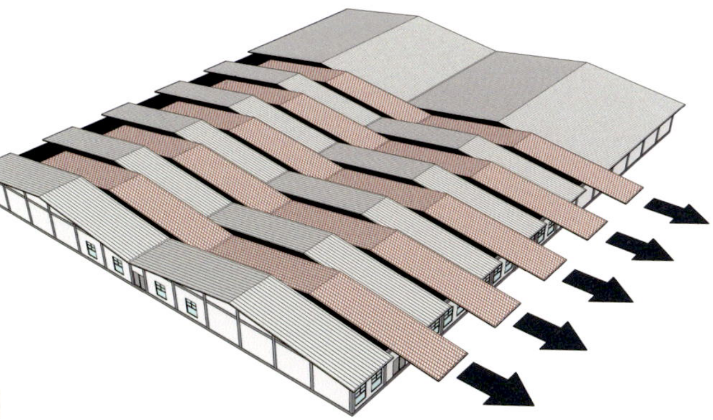

2

3D representation of the roof showing the alternation of the roof sections shifting sideways (in the same direction).

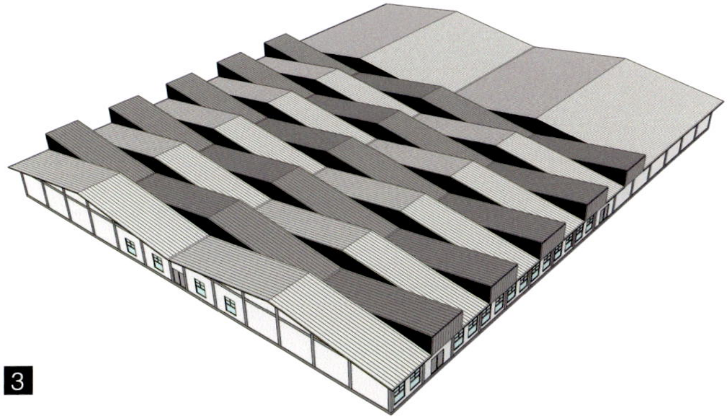

3

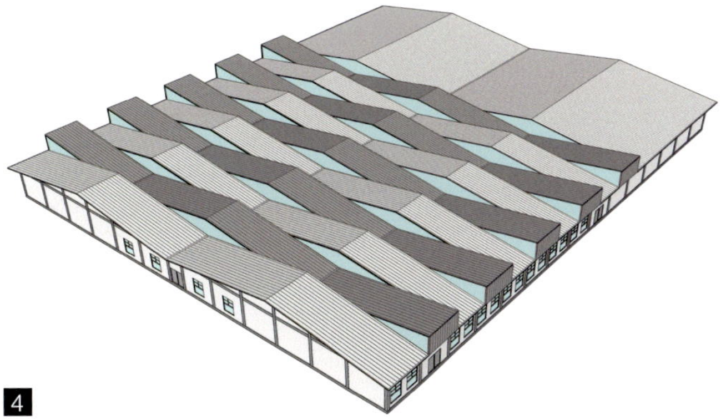

4

The diamond-shaped openings come into play when the shifting roof sections move by approximately 19 meters.

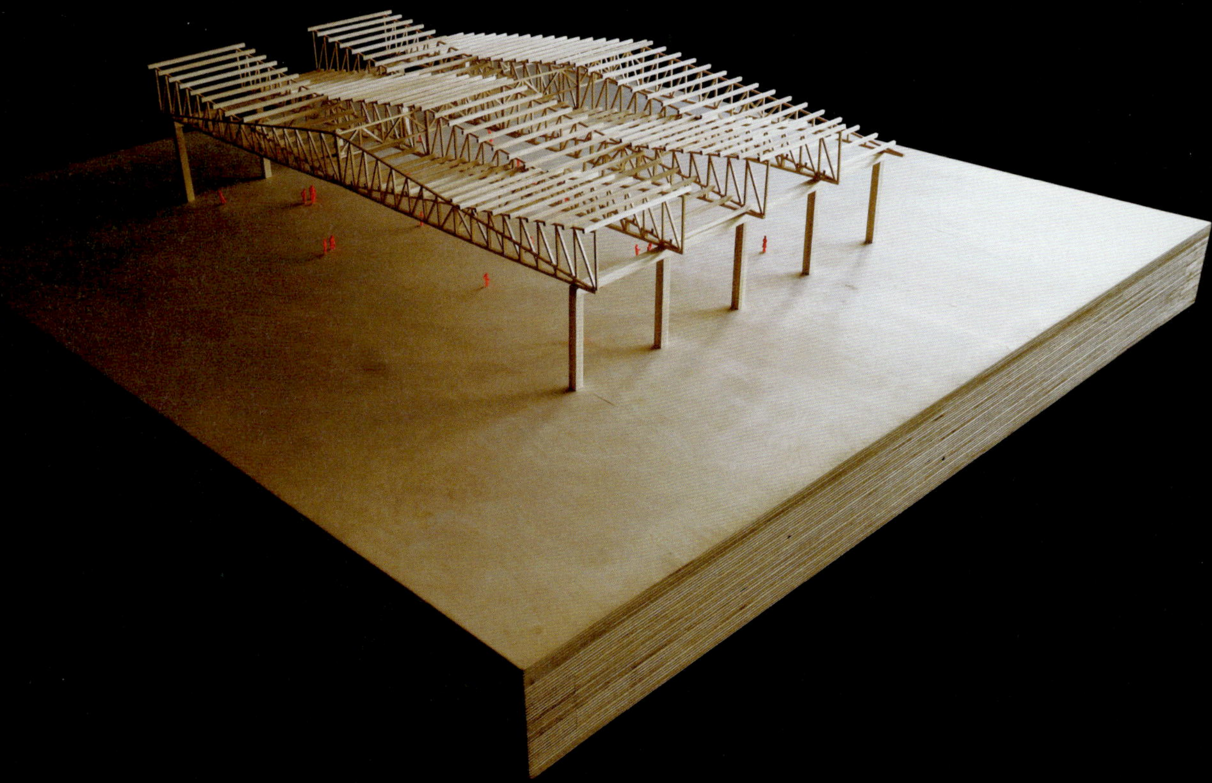

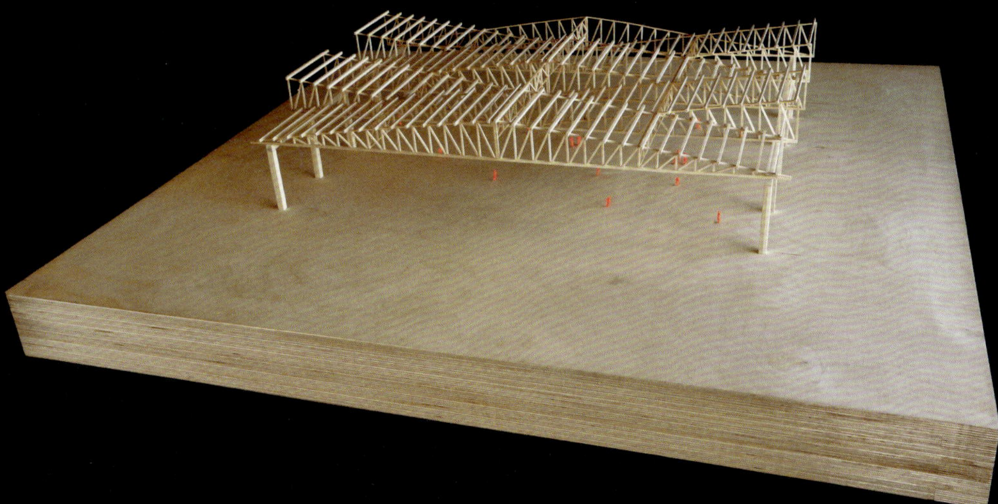

On site progress photo of the
erection of the roof structure.

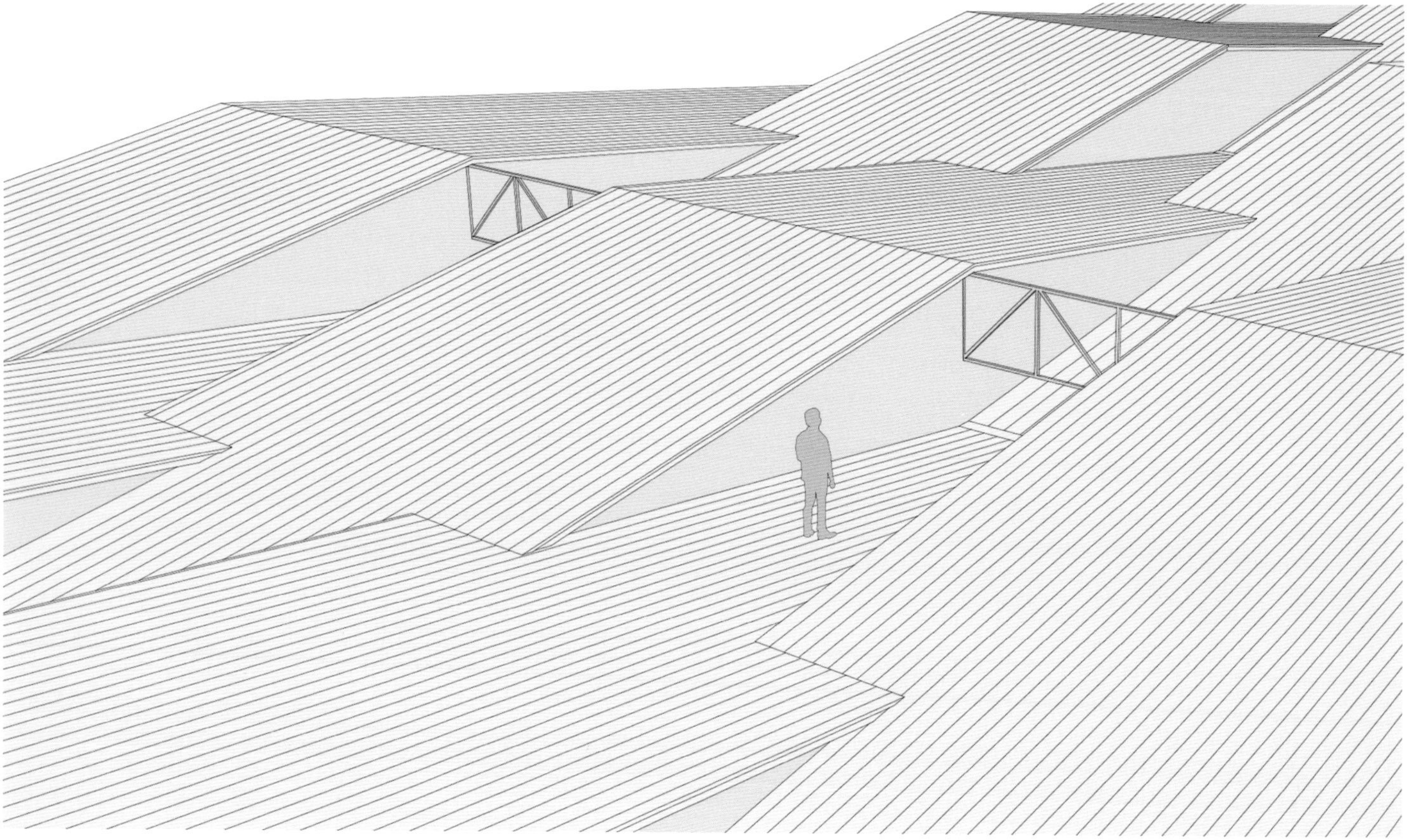

Above Exterior roof view.
Right Axonometric view of the roof structure.

Above Roof view showing the extent of the diamond-shaped skylights and roof structure.
Left Interior view of the facility showing the roof structure, the diamond-shaped skylights.

Muse Edition

This is an unusual project because it is an adaptive/ reuse project, dictated not by design, but by circumstance. The retail space occupies two floors. However, unlike the rest of K11 MUSEA, which is newly built, the premises of Muse Edition are housed within the bottom section of an existing three-story building from the 1970's, featuring a ballroom above and an open-air swimming pool on the rooftop, which are part of an adjacent hotel (The Regent) but under different ownership (from Muse Edition and K11 MUSEA). The period structures that we had to preserve include waffle ceilings (on two floors) and four steel columns at the double-height atrium space. Since both the waffle ceiling and the steel columns evoke an industrial character and a "machined aesthetic", we decided to celebrate this industrial sensibility in this retail project, which is rarely seen in Hong Kong. We designed a series of floating glass skins to not only protect and preserve the steel columns but also to display them (as if in a museum setting) simultaneously. The glass skins are skewed at an angle and taper from top to bottom to create a dramatic impression. The laminated glass panels are frameless and feature exposed corners for ease of maintenance. Natural light is nonexistent at this section of the shopping mall. Working together with a lighting designer, we incorporated a computer–controlled LED lighting system into the waffle ceiling of the double-height atrium space, which can modulate the interior lighting conditions to mimic the different times of day and seasonal variations. We created numerous nautical motifs to establish the required thematic linkage, ensuring compatibility with the client's designation of the entire development as "Victoria Dockside". **Rope** is used to clad columns and fire-shutter enclosures; **brass** connectors and fixtures, and **teak wood** are used on the staircase and balustrade; **copper conduits** are used on the exposed ceiling as directional guides, and also as electrical conduits for accent light fixtures throughout the ceiling; a series of **seashells** is embedded onto the concrete floor. This is our nuanced approach to integrating our project into the development's larger narrative.

Type

Retail Space (Shopping Mall)

Year

2018-2019

Area

1,860 sq.m (20,000 sq.ft.)

Material

Glass (Primary Building Material)

Address

Part of K11 MUSEA, Victoria Dockside, Kowloon, Hong Kong

Objective

To preserve and showcase the period structures within the 2-storey space; and to create a unique retail experience for the visitors.

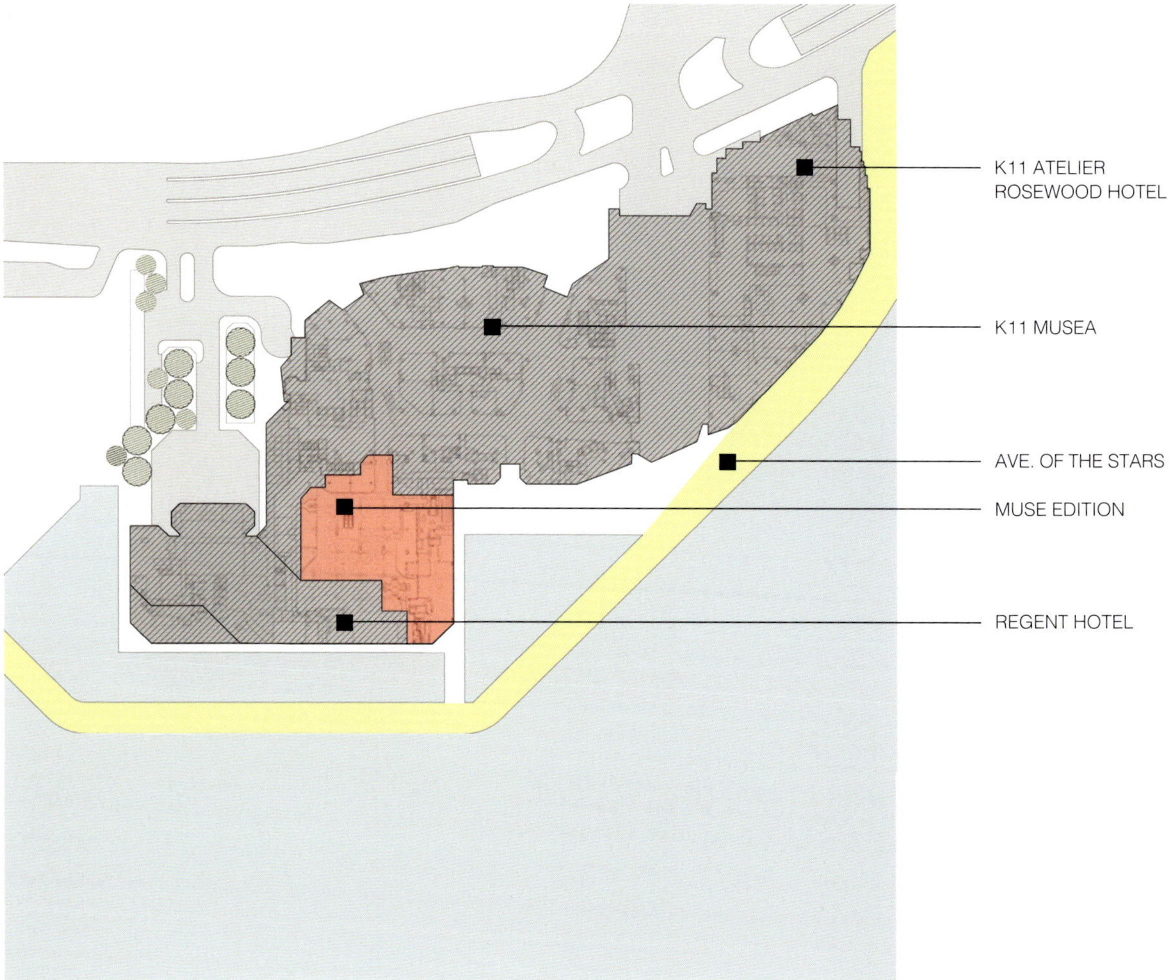
K11 ATELIER
ROSEWOOD HOTEL
K11 MUSEA
AVE. OF THE STARS
MUSE EDITION
REGENT HOTEL

SITE PLAN

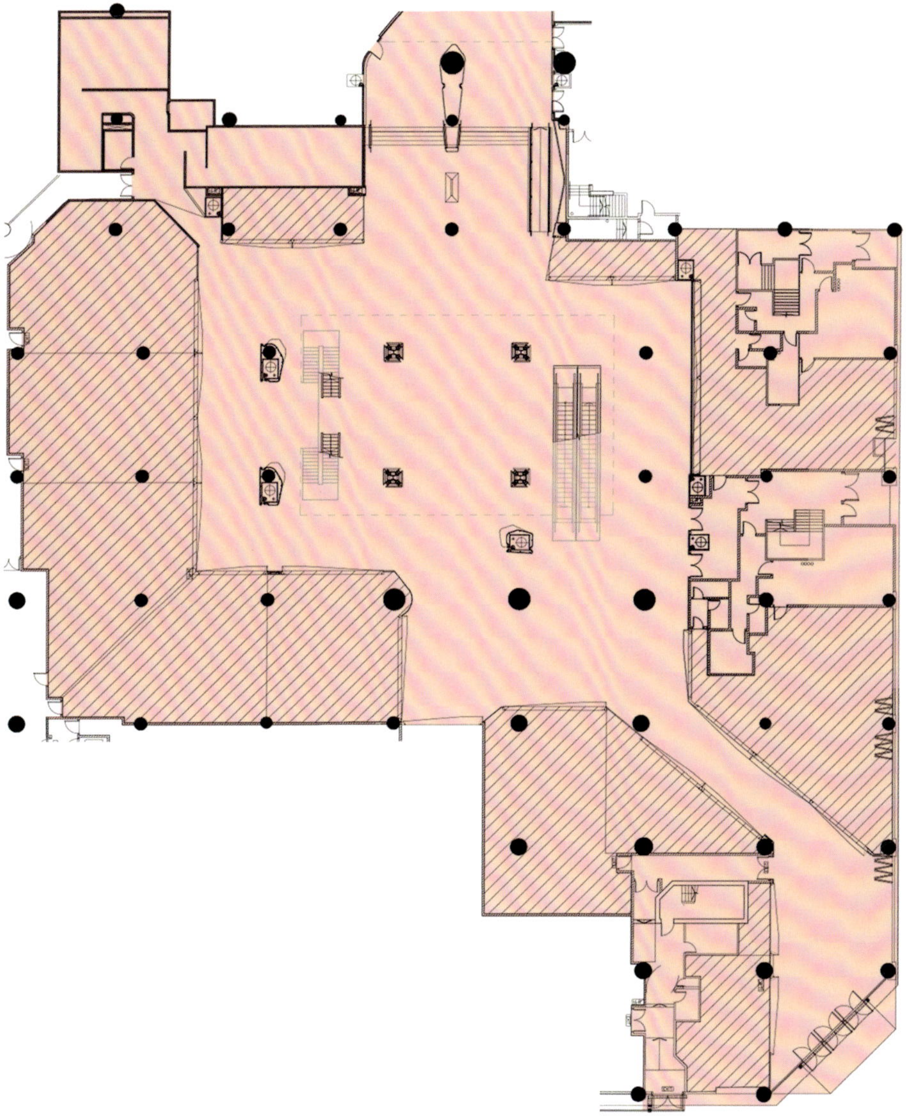

LAYOUT PLAN

On-site photos during our first site visit, prior to the commencement of the design process.

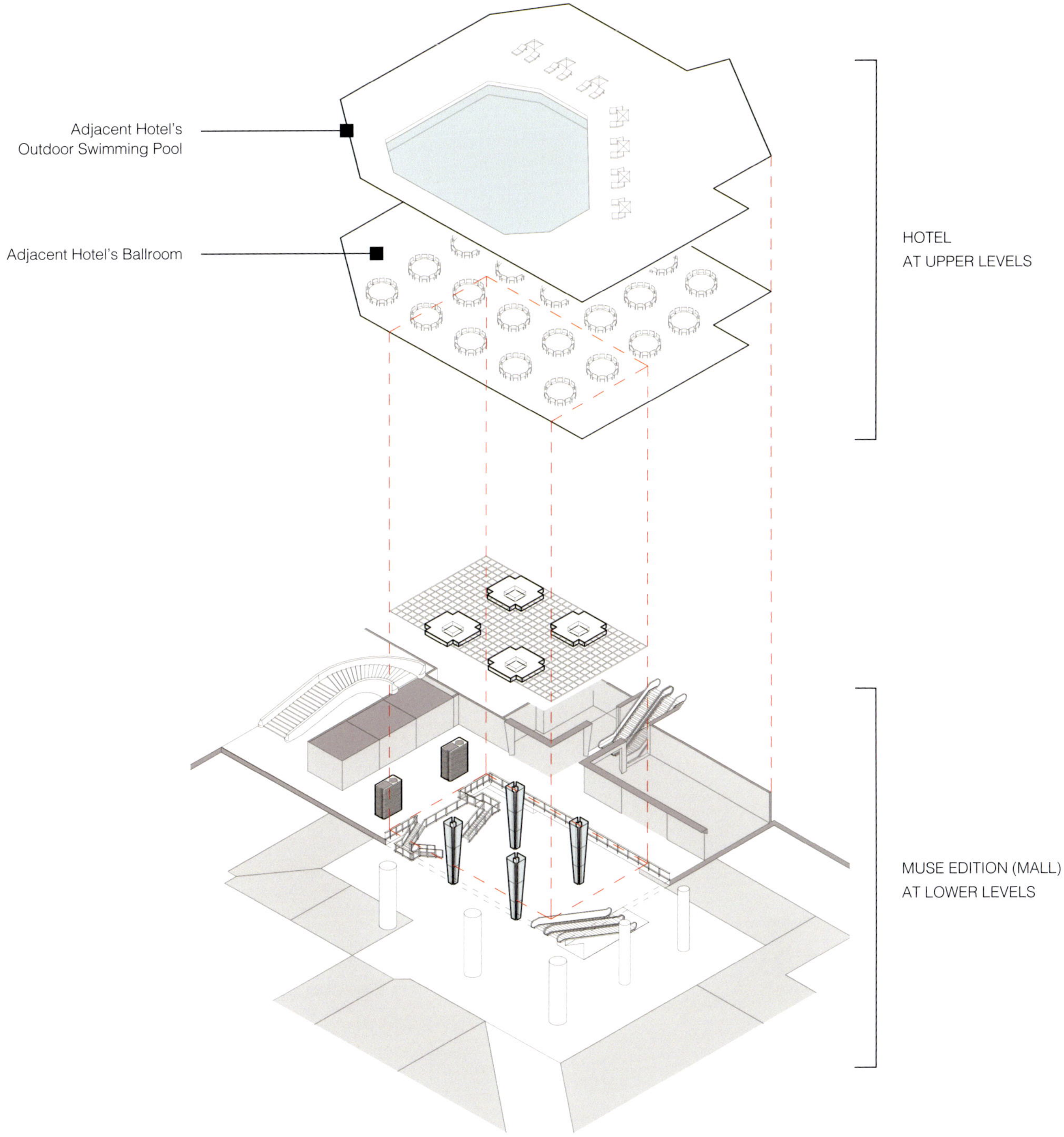
Adjacent Hotel's
Outdoor Swimming Pool
Adjacent Hotel's Ballroom
HOTEL
AT UPPER LEVELS
MUSE EDITION (MALL)
AT LOWER LEVELS

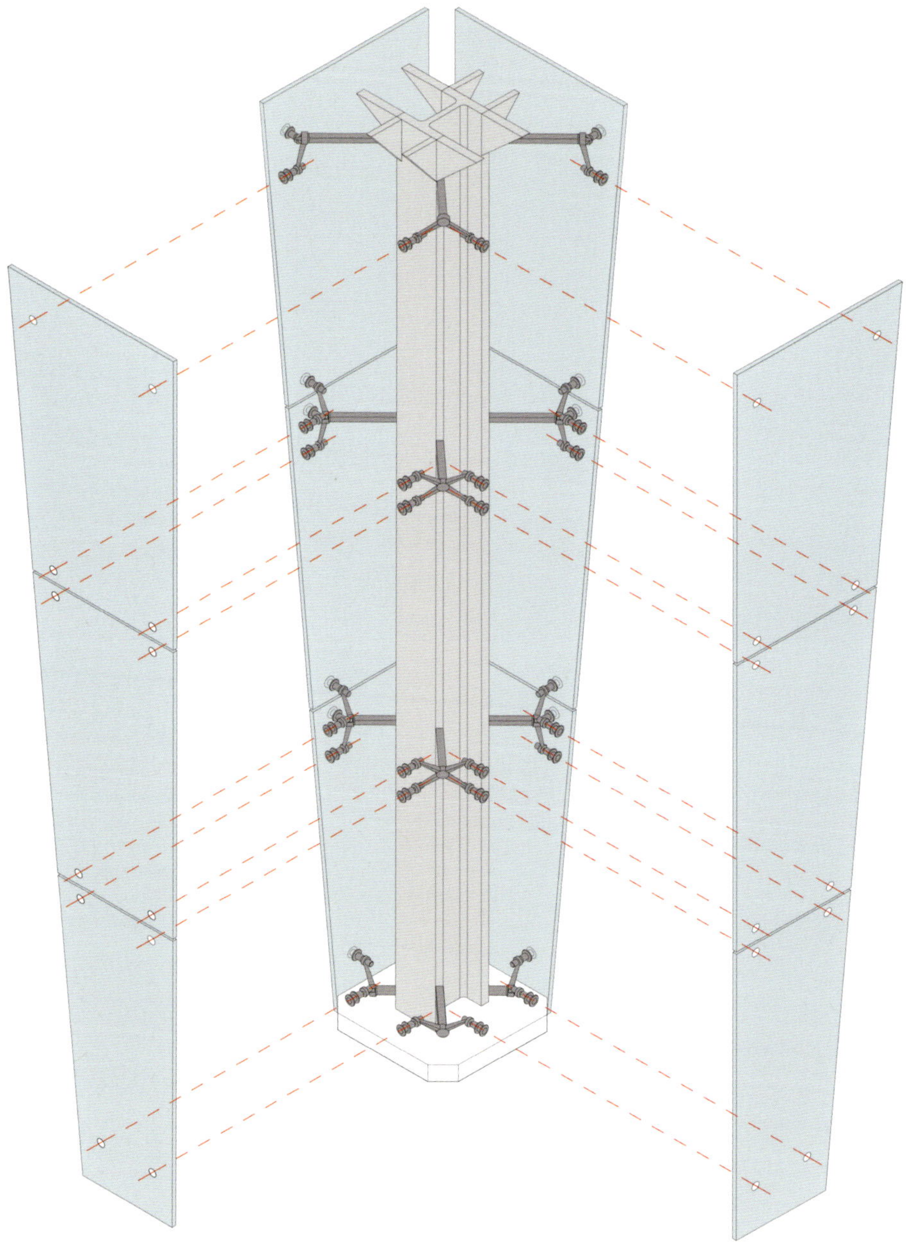

Exploded axonometric drawing of the steel column in relation to the glass skin, showing the extent of the "spider" supports along the length of the column.

Close-up details of the "spider" supports for the glass skins.

Above The column cap condition during our first site visit.
Next page The column cap condition with our intervention in place. Note that we actually extended the rhythm of the waffles surrounding the steel column, and specified mirror-finish stainless-steel for the column cap surfaces to give the illusion that the glass skin/ column continues upward.

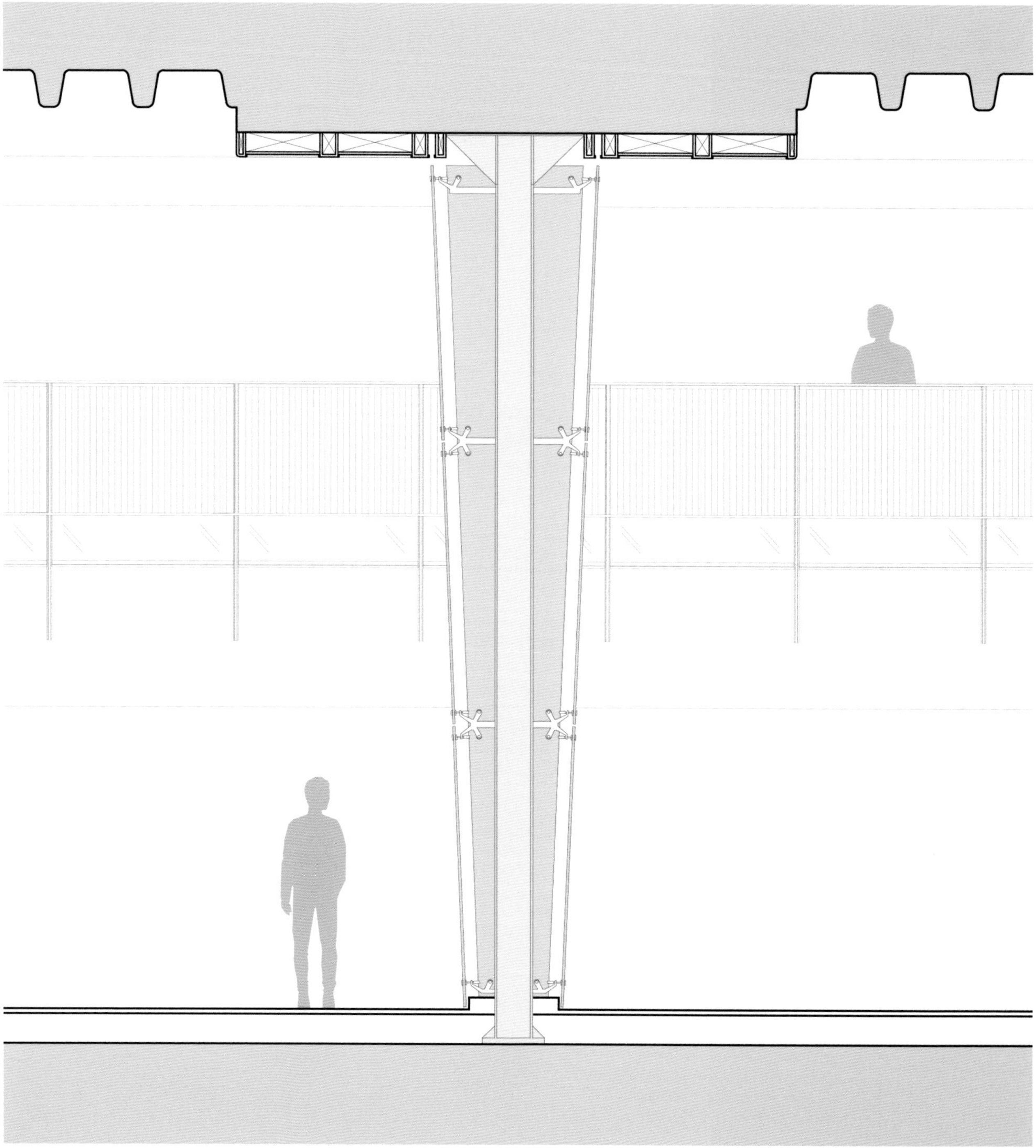

Real Life
is color you
can't control

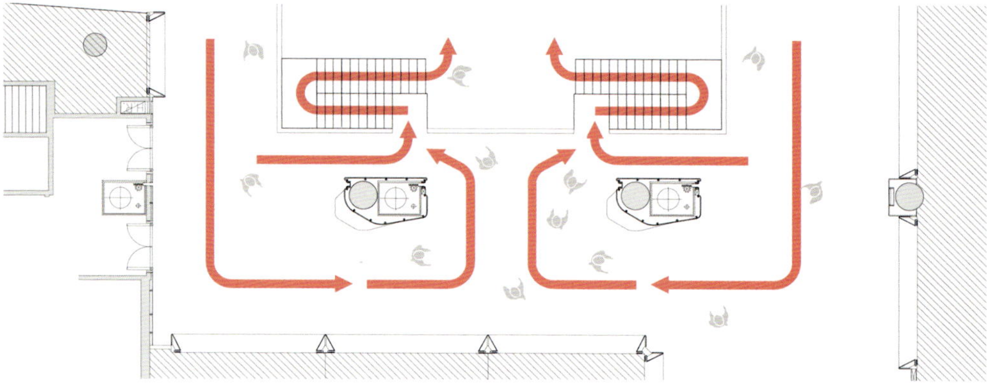

The client's original staircase layout,
with problematic circulation flow.

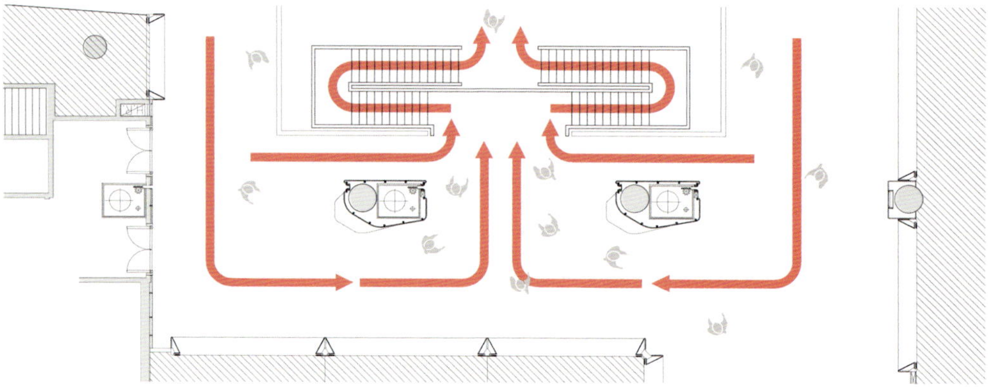

Our revised design for the staircase
which provides improved circulation flow.

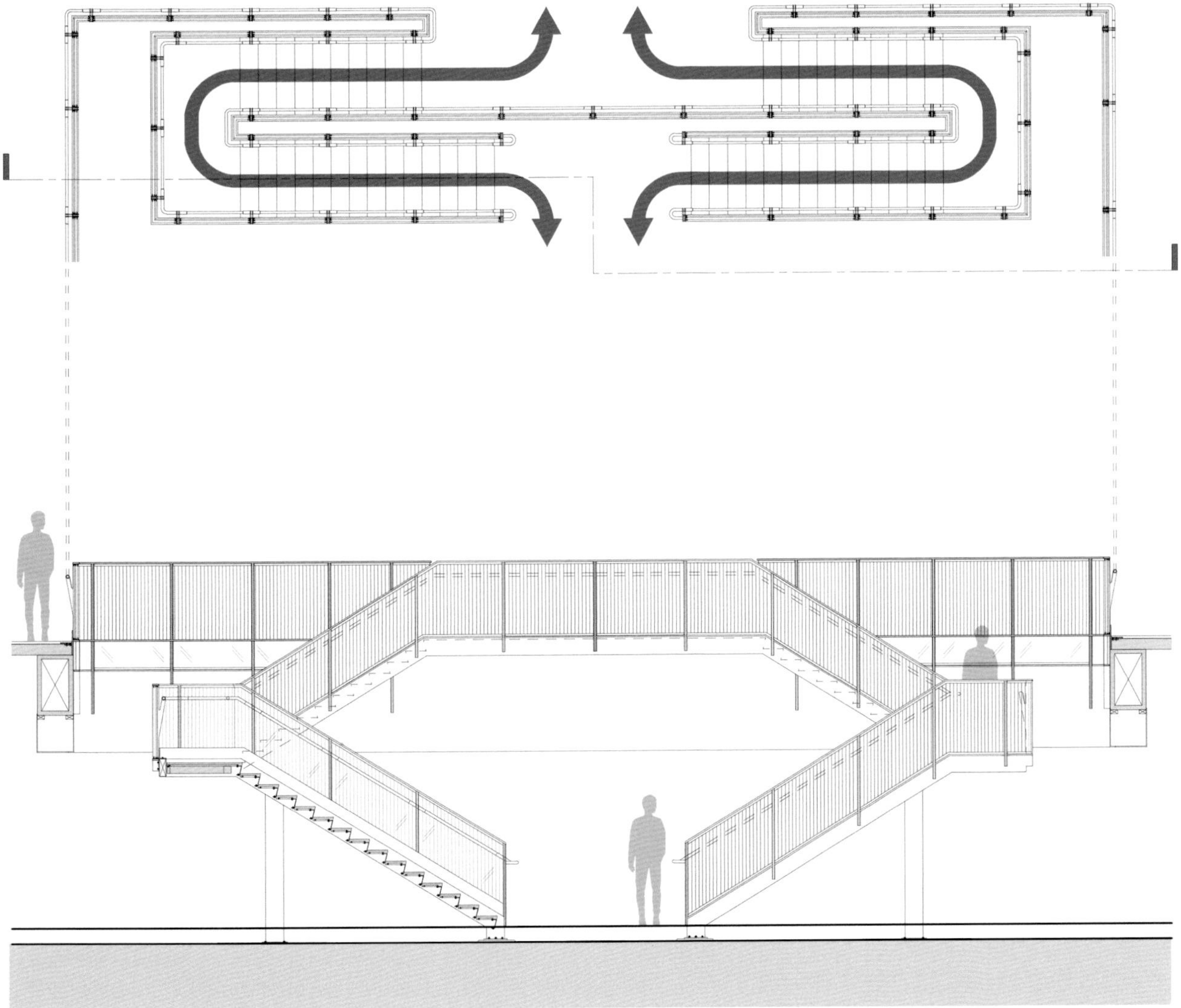

Left A partial view of the glass column in the foreground, with copper conduits, an LED display, the balustrade and the waffle ceiling in the background.
Right above Copper, a nautical element is specified for the conduits, that house the electrical wires for accent lights throughout the exposed ceiling. The copper conduits also act as a visual aid gulding people throughout the 2- storey space.
Right below Rope, another nautical element, is used as a cladding material in this project.

MUSE EDITION

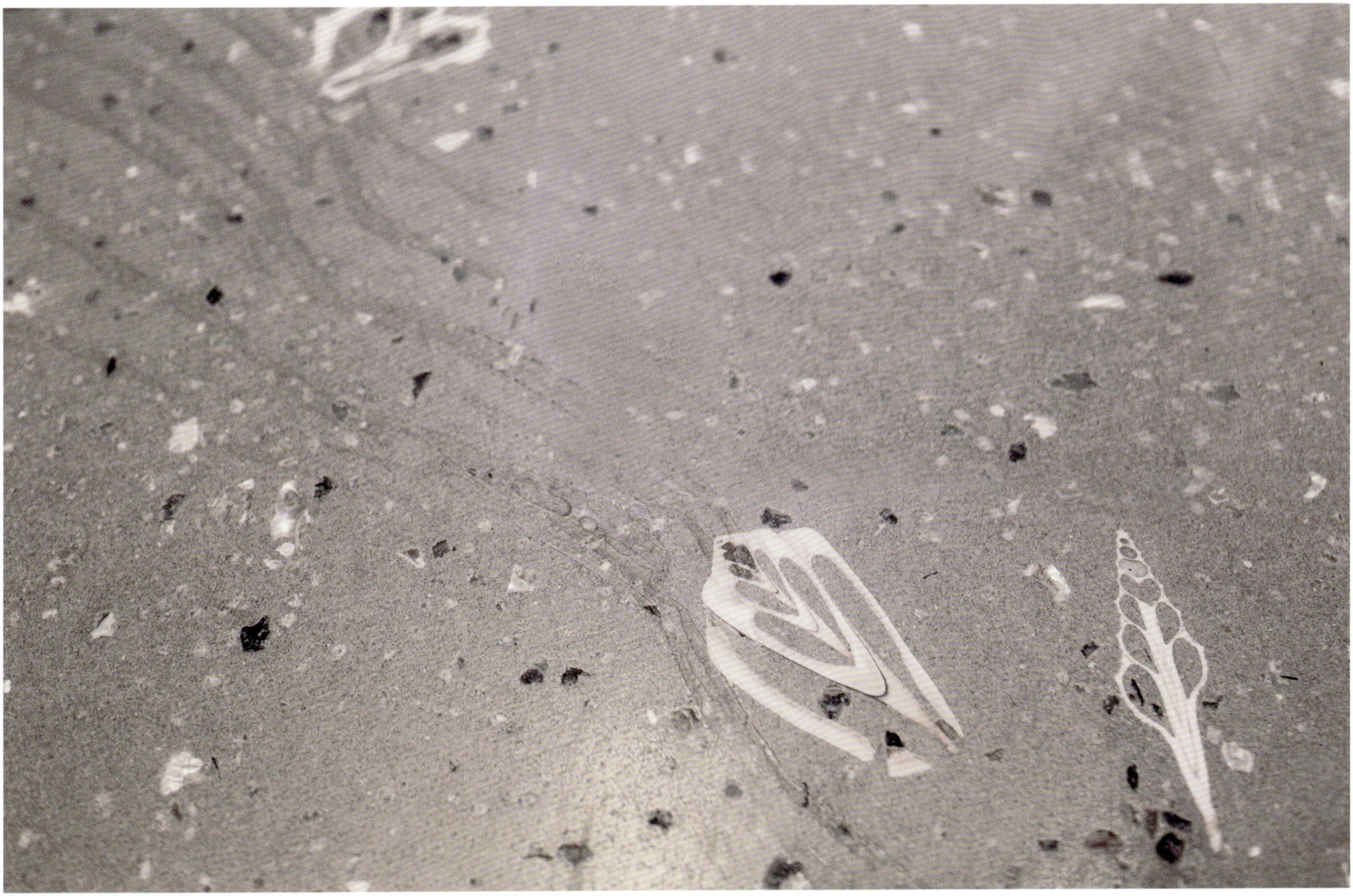

Seashells, another nautical motif, are embedded into the concrete floor. The nautical motifs in this project are used to establish the required thematic linkage, ensuring compatibility with the client's designation of the entire development as "Victoria Dockside".

Entrance Pavilion

The Entrance Pavilion is a security checkpoint for THANA CITY, Bangkok, Thailand. THANA CITY is a cluster of developments built over 20 years, comprising a golf and country club, a recently established international school, and various types of residences, including townhouses and condominiums. The project brief required a new identity for the front entrance, where the Entrance Pavilion is situated. The pavilion measures approximately 14 meters in height and 40 meters in width. The pavilion structure is constructed using cast-in-place reinforced concrete. Concrete is typically bulky and chunky. To create an inviting pavilion, we devised an undulating form to overcome the bulkiness and heaviness of concrete. Much of our energy was spent on detailing, dimensioning, and shaping the different parts of the portal. The tapering on the edge of the concrete was a key factor in the visual lightness of this 1,300+ ton structure. A series of lanterns is situated at the upper portions of the pavilion to create a different impression of the pavilion at night. Perforated stainless steel panels form the lantern enclosures. At one point, the client expressed concerns about the 50 mm diameter specification for the perforations on the stainless-steel panels. They were afraid that birds would get into the lanterns to create nests within, which would be a nightmare to maintain. To address this concern, we added a thin layer of stainless-steel "chicken wire" behind the stainless-steel panels to keep out the birds, but more importantly, maintain our desired level of transparency for the lanterns, especially when viewed from a distance at night. A linear LED light strip is embedded into the outer concrete edge of the pavilion, highlighting its undulating form. A water fountain is placed in front of the pavilion, dividing the traffic that enters and exits. Illuminated graphics of "THANA CITY" sit right above the water level on the fountain, creating interesting reflections at night.

Type

Entrance Security Checkpoint

Year

2019-2020

Area

2,500 sq.m

Material

Cast-in-place Reinforced Concrete

Address

THANA CITY, Bang Na, Trat, Thailand

Objective

To create a new identity for THANA CITY and an inviting structure for visitors, residents, and other patrons.

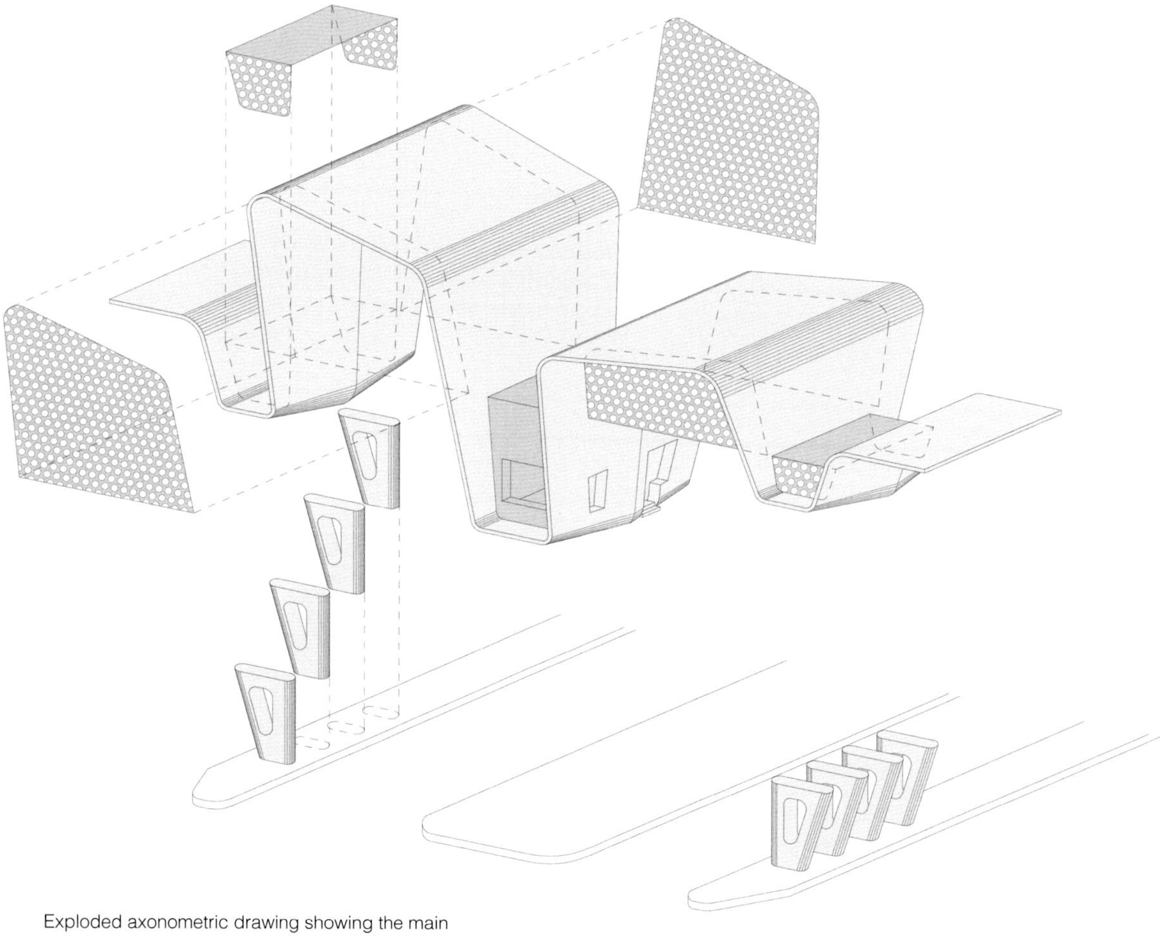

Exploded axonometric drawing showing the main components in concrete and perforated stainless-steel.

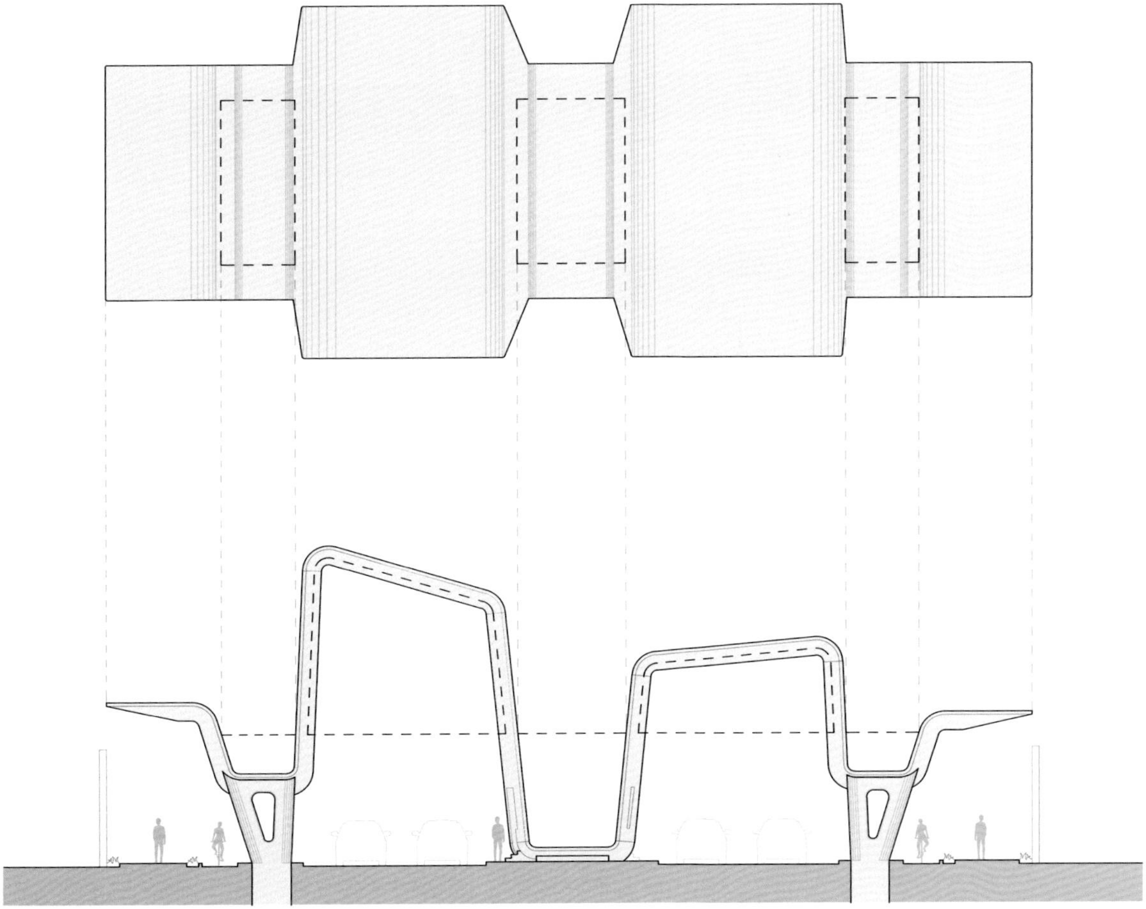

Roof Plan and Section of the pavilion.

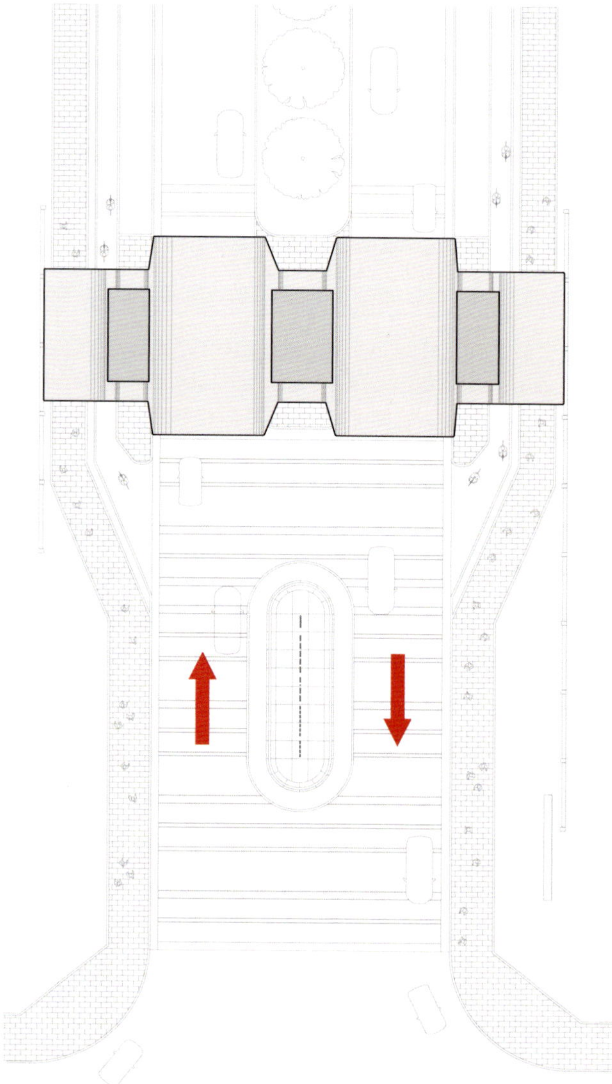

ROOF PLAN

Progress photo during construction.

More progress photos during construction.

View of the pavilion after the
formwork has been removed.

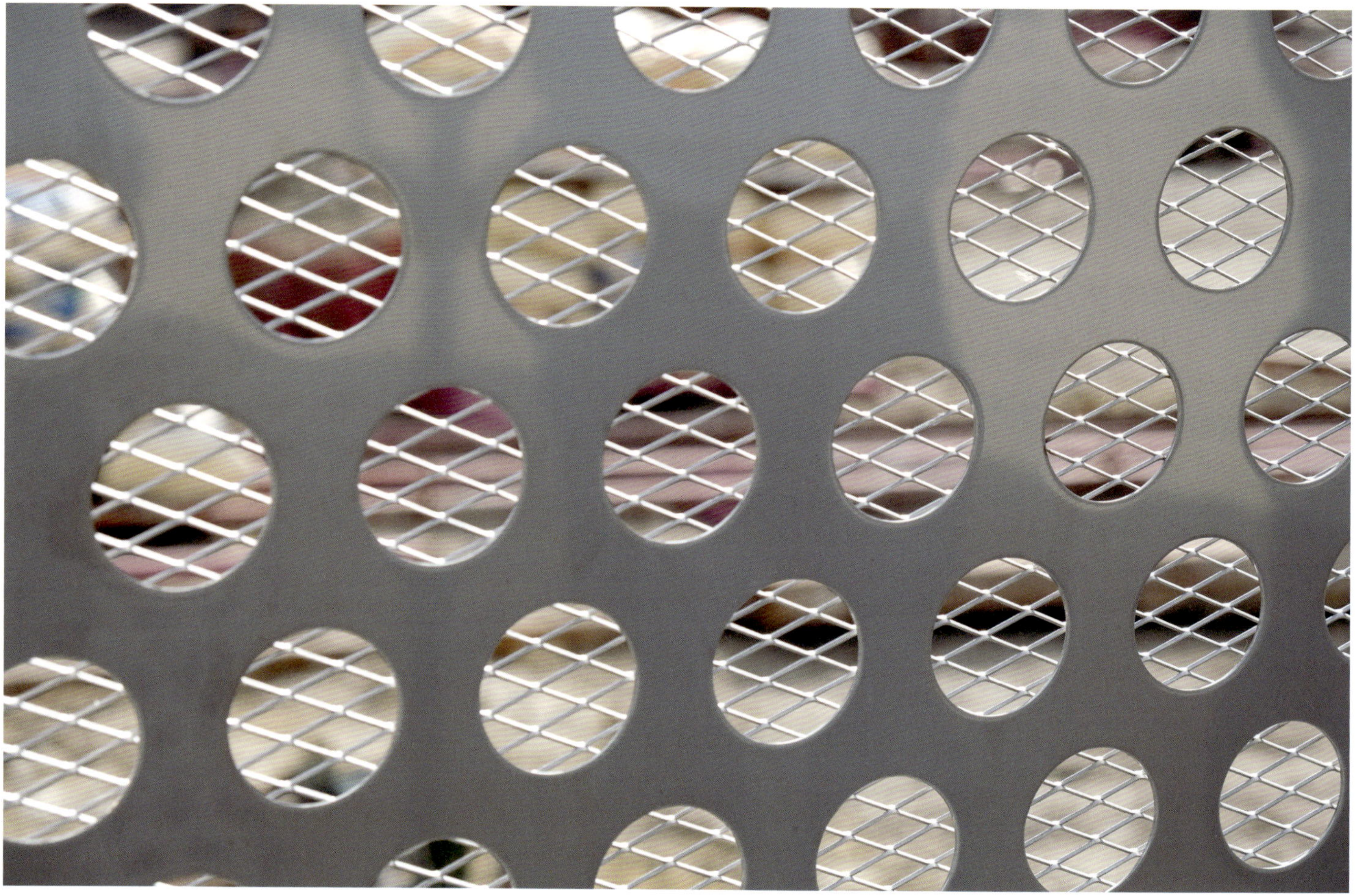

A mock-up of the perforated stainless-steel with the "chicken wire" behind to keep the birds out.

A close-up view of the edge of the concrete showing the tapering effect and the perforated stainless-steel panels of the lantern (daytime).

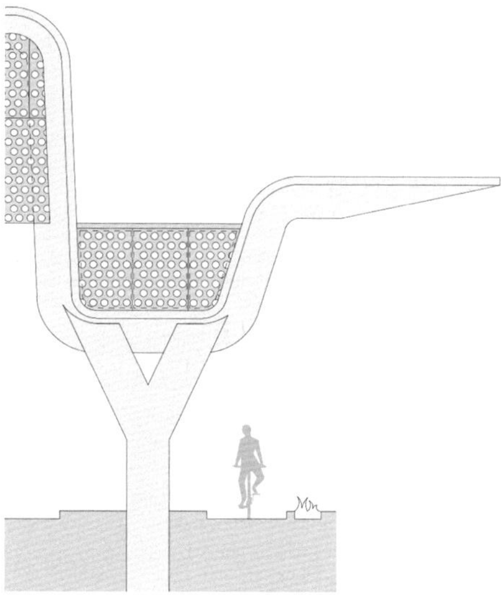

Structural engineer's original structural base design.

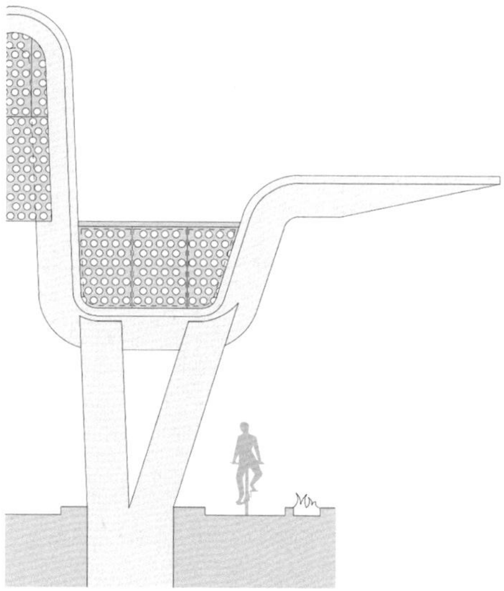

Evolution of the base design.

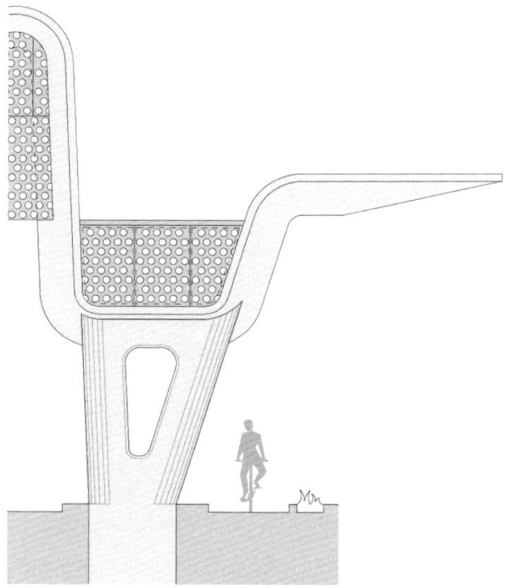

Revised and final structural base.

THANA

Afterword

Gene Miao
Founder and Principal Designer, Studio 1:1

Like many young architects, I started my career with interior projects, as this was the easiest way to enter the industry. I carried out projects that included fit-outs for apartments, retail shops, corporate offices, clinics, and even a dog spa. This work was plentiful in Hong Kong, and paid the bills, but it did not give me a sense of accomplishment or achievement. Deep down, I wanted to work on larger-scale projects or more groundbreaking work that I had imagined while pursuing my degree. And yet, the economics of property development in a densely packed city like Hong Kong, where land is money, meant that these projects would likely be located elsewhere, in countries with more abundant land and a different property dynamic.

Since 2016, I have been fortunate enough to work on larger-scale projects, one each in Thailand, the Philippines, and Hong Kong. If the first phase of my career was interior work, I would consider these three projects as the core of the second phase, where I was able to carve out space from the humdrum interior work to pursue and execute projects with a more deliberate footprint.

This book is thus a celebration of the three projects that have helped me step towards my architectural vision. With these larger-scale projects, many socio-economic factors, in addition to the usual programmatic, geographical, technological, and cultural variables, are at play, adding to the complexity and challenges that must be resolved. Many stars needed to align to bring each of these projects to life. For a small practice with limited resources, it is no small feat. And I am grateful to all the clients, collaborators, and consultants that we have worked with to execute them.

Back when I was a student of architecture, we would create physical drawings and models to represent and test our ideas in scaled-down formats—for instance, a model in 1:100 scale or a plan drawing in 1:500 scale. (Today, these are mostly rendered on a computer.) In this light, 1:1 scale refers to a representation of something in its full, exact life size. To me, this can also represent the actual project. In the spirit of 1:1, I intentionally did not include any unbuilt work in this book. We have projects at various stages of conception, and we are eagerly awaiting the day when these, too, can be executed in 1:1.

We have chosen the name “Architecture under the Radar” deliberately. Radar is an acronym for Radio Detection and Ranging, a system that uses radio waves to detect and locate objects such as an aircraft. During World War II, military pilots began using radar technology to detect enemy aircraft and ships. In response, pilots on the opposing side would fly at low altitudes to avoid radar detection. This tactic was called “flying under the radar.”The expression gradually found its way into everyday language as a metaphor for avoiding detection or staying out of the public eye.

“Architecture Under the Radar” seeks to explore architectural endeavors that have quietly existed, often escaping the scrutiny and appreciation of both the architectural community and the general public. And while we can “explain” this phenomenon in social, economic or other terms, we should also understand what we may be missing by glazing over these projects. During the Covid era, we lost three years: things just ceased to progress, both in terms of construction that was stalled, but also ideas that lay unexplored as we urgently dealt with other matters. Today, many are striving to reclaim lost opportunities or to regain the search for fulfillment. This, too is a background to this book.

Through the pages of this book, we aim to illuminate these lesser-known projects and foster a greater understanding of our contributions to the field. We invite both the general and specialist audiences to engage with our perspective, cultivating an even broader discourse on architecture.

Project Credits

Light & Span

Program
Manufacturing Facility

Client
FCF Manufacturing Corporation

Location
Mariveles, Bataan, The Philippines

Project Team
Gene Miao, Peter Lam, Chan Ching Wai

Construction
R.B. Ombao Construction

Photography
Edmon Leong, Gene Miao

Award
ARCHITECTURE MASTERPRIZE
2020 (Winner)

Muse Edition

Program
Retail Space (Shopping Mall)

Client
New World Development Company Ltd.

Location
K11 MUSEA, Victoria Dockside,
Kowloon, Hong Kong

Project Team
Gene Miao, Chan Ching Wai, Peter Lam

Lighting Consultants
Speirs & Major

Construction
New World Construction Company Ltd.

Photography
Xu Liang Leon, Joel Joa, Gene Miao

Award
Architizer A+ Award 2020 (Winner)

Entrance Pavilion

Program
Security Checkpoint

Client
BTS Group

Location
THANA CITY, Bang Na, Trat, Thailand

Project Team
Gene Miao, Chan Ching Wai

Lighting Consultant
Bo Steiber (Bangkok)

Structural Engineer
Meinhardt (Thailand) Ltd.

Construction
HHT Construction Co. Ltd.

Photography
Weerapon Singnoi

Awards
The PLAN Award 2022 (Finalist)
d/a (design anthology) Award 2021 (Finalist)

Gene Miao

Gene Miao is the Founder and Principal Designer of Studio 1:1, a Hong Kong-based emerging studio founded in 2006. The practice initially focused on residential, retail, and corporate interior projects, and since 2016 has undertaken larger-scale civic, commercial, and industrial projects across Asia. Studio 1:1 continues to refine its vision, merging aspects of innovative design with a strong community-based and sustainability-focused grounding.

The Studio has received international architectural awards, including the Architecture MasterPrize and Architizer A+ Award; its work has also been shortlisted for the PLAN Award and d/a (Design Anthology) Award.

In addition to his role with Studio 1:1, Gene is engaged personally in a number of community and cultural projects in and around Hong Kong. His dedication to preserving local culture resulted in his founding “Day- Tau- Chung” (neighborhood worm), an online platform promoting and building awareness of lesser-known businesses, cultural sites, and other urban narratives with intangible cultural value. In 2008, Gene received PERSPECTIVE Magazine’s 40 Under 40 Award for ‘Design Activism’ for Day- Tau- Chung.

Gene received his Bachelor of Architecture and Bachelor of Fine Arts degrees from RISD (The Rhode Island School of Design) and worked in New York City for a number of years before returning to Hong Kong to build his practice. He continues to explore how design can shape the way commerce is carried out, as well as guide users through concepts of social value, community, and heritage.

Nader Tehrani

For his "contributions to architecture as an art", Nader Tehrani is the recipient of The American Academy of Arts and Letters' Arnold W. Brunner Memorial Prize, the highest form of recognition of artistic merit in the United States. With nineteen Progressive Architecture Awards, he is also an elected member of the American Academy of Arts and Sciences, the National Academy of Design, and recipient of the Design Visionary Award from the Cooper Hewitt-Smithsonian Design Museum. Tehrani is the Founding Principal of NADAAA, an interdisciplinary practice with works across scales from infrastructure to urbanism, architecture, and installations. The former Head of the Department of Architecture at MIT (2010-14), Tehrani was also Dean of The Irwin S. Chanin School of Architecture of The Cooper Union (2015-22). Widely exhibited at MOMA, LA MOCA and the Venice Biennale, NADAAA's work is also in the permanent collections of the Nasher Sculpture Center and the Canadian Centre for Architecture.

Book Credits

Graphic Design: Florencia Damilano

Editorial Director: Caroline Kipling

Art Direction: Oscar Riera Ojeda

Copy Editing: Kit Maude

Studio 1:1
www.studio1-1.hk
info@studio1-1.hk

OSCAR RIERA OJEDA
PUBLISHERS

ISBN 978-1-964490-17-5
Published by Oscar Riera Ojeda Publishers Limited
Printed in China

Oscar Riera Ojeda Publishers Limited
Unit 1331, Beverley Commercial Centre,
87-105 Chatham Road South, Tsim Sha Tsui, Kowloon, Hong Kong

Production Offices
Suit 19, Shenyun Road,
Nanshan District, Shenzhen 518055, China

International Customer Service & Editorial Questions: +1-484-502-5400

www.oropublishers.com | www.oscarrieraojeda.com
oscar@oscarrieraojeda.com